Tweet This!

Twitter for Business

Jessica Miller-Merrell

Tweet This!
Twitter for Business

For updates and to learn more about the latest
information and news about Twitter as well as other
social media platforms, visit my Web site at:
www.tweetingmybusiness.com

For updates and information surrounding this book, follow:
www.twitter.com/tweetthis

Manufactured in the United States of America.

For information, please contact:

The P3 Press
16200 North Dallas Parkway, Suite 170
Dallas, Texas 75248

www.thep3press.com
972-248-9500
A New Era in Publishing™

ISBN-13: 978-1-933651-66-8
ISBN-10: 1-933651-66-0
LCCN: 2009911583

Author contact information:

Jessica Miller-Merrell
Follow me on Twitter at:
www.twitter.com/blogging4jobs

To my husband, Greg,
and Baby Ryleigh.

Table of Contents

Preface

Over the course of my career, I have used tools such as chat rooms, blogs, Myspace, Facebook, LinkedIn, and Twitter as a form of communication and as a way to inexpensively recruit candidates and promote events. Because I have been a relatively early adopter, friends, colleagues, and businesses have looked to me to help them leverage these online tools to recruit employees and grow their business.

Fast-forward to December 2008: my husband, Greg, and I were nine months pregnant with our first child. It was late morning when my water broke on December 12, and I posted on Twitter the following: "My water broke. Heading to the hospital." When Ryleigh came into the world very early the next morning, we announced her arrival through both Twitter and Facebook. Over the course of 2009, Twitter became my place to engage others, seek comfort, and build and grow both business and personal relationships. In April of this year, when my husband lost his father, I turned to Twitter to find comfort with my virtual support network.

Since I first logged on to Twitter in the summer of 2008, it has grown and changed dramatically. Quantcast.com estimates that from October 2008 to September 2009 Twitter's traffic grew from 5 million users to 27 million in the United States alone. Facebook, another popular social media platform, boasts more users than some small countries with over 100 million in the United States. Even still, businesses are most surprised by the fact that the largest growth for both these platforms comes from the 35- to 50-year-old demographic and not the 18–34 crowd.

The concept of *Tweet This!* was developed during the first few weeks after Ryleigh was brought into this world. I was on maternity leave from my corporate job. It became clear during my time off that there was a need for a Twitter business resource for the small- to medium-sized business, entrepreneur, and consultant. With that in mind, over the course of several months I began working on a Twitter manual which then quickly became a book. I hope that you will find *Tweet This!* to be an easy-to-read resource for the beginning to advanced Twitter user. I have worked hard to provide a variety of case studies that emphasize the importance of time management and getting the most out of Twitter for the small business. The strategies discussed have been tested by a number of business owners and experts, including me.

I hope that you will find this book, and Twitter, to be valuable resources to grow and shape your business. My book has led my family and me on an incredible journey that has resulted in me leaving the corporate world, realizing my own dream, and starting my own consulting practice.

So sit back and enjoy *Tweet This!*

Acknowledgments

This book couldn't have happened without so many people. I'd like to recognize and thank, first and foremost, my wonderful family: my husband, Greg, who supports me in whatever I do; my daughter, Ryleigh, now ten months old, who has forever changed our lives in so many ways; my parents, Terry and Leigh; and my sisters, Jamie and Julie, and their families. I love you all! I also want to thank my in-laws, Barney and Shirley, who taught me to live and love every day. Barney, you will never be forgotten. I've appreciated everyone's help and support in so many ways.

After my family, I'd like to thank a list of amazing and special people who helped me do this: Irma's Burgers, Bill Vick, Dave Gardner (who also served as a case study and editor), Sheri Guyse, Becky McCray, Matt Galloway, Mark Stelzner, Samuel Gordon's Jewelers, Daniel Gordon, Ryan Parrott, Trichology Salon, Greg Welchel, The Oklahoma Gazette, Chris Wilson, Eddie Roach, Sharlyn Lauby, Giovanni Gallucci, Angelika Movie Theatres, Latoicha Givens, Brian Blake, Kevin Jessop, My Workster, Oklahoma Humane Society, Harvey Jenkins, and Edmond Active.

And finally, I'd like to thank my publisher, the P3 Press, who helped me make my dream a reality. Cynthia Stillar did an amazing job of keeping me focused and had a great eye for detail.

To everyone, I am deeply grateful.

What is Twitter?

Twitter was a service originally created for friends, family, and co-workers to communicate and stay connected through the exchange of quick, frequent answers to one simple question: What are you doing? It was originally developed for use with SMS text messaging. Twitter users post *tweets*—posts written in 140 characters or fewer.

Think of Twitter as a virtual cocktail party or water cooler. It is a place where people come to get to know each other and stay connected and up-to-date on the latest news and information. I use Twitter to promote my new blog posts, upcoming seminars, and articles I have written. I also use it to develop new relationships and follow those within my industry or others that I admire. Twitter can be used a thousand different ways for a thousand different reasons.

Here are some common uses for Twitter:

- *Twitter users stay connected with friends and family members.*
- *Bloggers use Twitter as a mini-blogging tool.*
- *Businesses use Twitter as a customer service platform for public relations, brand management, and as a marketing tool.*
- *Developers use Twitter to make API Tools of their own.*
- *Job seekers use Twitter to find unadvertised jobs.*
- *Business professionals and recruiters use Twitter to find leads and candidates.*
- *Some use Twitter as a source of breaking news and information.*

Picture yourself driving on the highway as you make your way on your morning commute. As you weave in and out of traffic surrounded by thousands of other morning commuters, a billboard sign grabs your attention. The Hard Rock Café is coming to your town. You make a mental note to yourself to visit the Hard Rock Café Web site when you arrive at work. Later that morning after checking e-mails and voice-mails, you visit the Hard Rock Café Web site and casually mention it to several of your co-workers in person and by e-mail. Word quickly spreads throughout your office and circle of friends, and by the end of the day, the new Hard Rock Café is the talk of the town and among your family, co-workers, and friends.

Twitter is exactly like that. It's a virtual highway or stream of information called the Twitter Stream. Twitter users weave in and out of the stream of information. Someone's "billboard," or tweet, grabs a Twitter user's attention, causing dialogue between Twitizens—also known as Twitter citizens—leading them to a Web site mentioned within a tweet or the user's bio.

Restaurants and companies like the Hard Rock Café use Twitter as a way to inform the Twitter Stream of new information and develop relationships with their customers directly. One restaurant local to the Oklahoma City area that has had success in using Twitter to promote their business is Irma's Burger Shack. Irma's Burger Shack has two locations and uses their Twitter account, @irmasburgers, to tweet their lunch specials and engage their customers. In

July 2009, @irmasburgers boasted 656 followers, certainly not a large number in comparison to other national chains like @pizzahut which has over 14,000 followers. Irma's Burgers began using Twitter in January 2009. Their success story centers around selling out their lunch special in just 45 minutes after sending a tweet out on Twitter. Lunch special tweets are now sent out daily.

Using This Book

This book has been created and formatted with small businesses, consultants, and nonprofits in mind. Modeled after my own Twitter for Business class—also called "Tweet This!"—this book takes into consideration the time and immediacy that business professionals face when choosing to make the jump onto the social media platform, Twitter. Because business professionals can use Twitter thousands of different ways, I've chosen to feature a variety of businesses from a diverse group of industries. Use these case studies to help develop your business's Twitter strategy to market, grow, promote, and develop an online presence.

At the back of this book is an appendix with helpful tools and worksheets to organize your creative thoughts, goals, and ideas while creating your Twitter business plan. Don't wait to log onto Twitter until the conclusion of this book. Dive right in and enjoy *Tweet This!*

History of Twitter

In 2006, a think tank company called Obvious Corporation, formerly known as Odeo Corp., created Twitter. The concept behind Twitter was born during a day-long brainstorming session focused on reinventing the company. The brainchild behind Twitter was @jack, also known as Jack Dorsey. And it was during this brainstorming session that @jack described a dispatch service that connects people to each other by phone through using text messaging. Work on the project began in March 2006. Twitter was created as a way to communicate using a social media platform derived from SMS—text messaging—and was originally called "Twttr." While SMS text messaging allows for 160 characters for each text message, @jack and his team decided upon 140 characters so the remaining 20 characters within the text message could be used for the Twitter account holder's username.

Twitter has been in the news everywhere these days. ESPN uses Twitter during sporting events to provide live real-time information from commentators and reporters. CNN and Ashton Kutcher's race to one million followers caused a media circus surrounding Twitter. Fans flocked to the site in April 2009 after Oprah announced her new Twitter account to her television show viewers on April 17. Her announcement led to a 37 percent increase in new visitors to the Twitter.com site in a single day. As of April 2009, Twitter had secured $57 million in funding from venture capitalists but had not yet made any profit.

User Demographics

Twitter's user and account data, including demographics, is hard to quantify. Quantcast, a company created in 2006, provides free direct-measurement of audiences for Web sites, blogs, videos, games, widgets, and all forms of online content. Quantcast helps businesses and marketers quantify the real-time social and digital media consumer information to accurately measure traffic and inferred audience data using a team of engineers and mathematicians. According to Quantcast's data in June 2009, Twitter's estimated Web site traffic in the United States is 26.5 million. Twitter users have the following demographics:

- Females make up 55% of Twitter users
- 43% of users are 18–34 years old
- 30% of users are 35–49 years old
- 19% of users are 50+ years old
- 29% of users' average income is $30–60K
- 43% of users have a college education
- 78% of users are Caucasian
- 11% of users are African-American
- 26% of users' average income is greater than $100K

Study after study from companies like Complete and Quantcast tell us that Twitter is not just for young twenty-something college students and teenagers texting and Facebooking. Twitter's audience includes a large percetage of educated, experienced, and influential professionals who are using the service as a way to connect, network, further strengthen business relationships, develop their own personal brand, and grow their business.

Bill Vick from Dallas, Texas, uses Twitter and other social media platforms as a way to drive traffic to his Web sites as well as to stay up-to-date on the latest recruiting and social media trends. Bill's background is very eclectic—he has previously worked for Fortune 500 companies in the fields of marketing, sales, and recruiting before starting the first of many businesses. Bill's current company, Vick & Associates, focuses on recruiting as well as educating job seekers and recruiters alike on using social media and other such tools to find candidates or jobs. Bill has two separate Twitter accounts he uses to promote four of his Web sites—billvick.com, xtremerecruiting.tv, sixfigurecareercoaching.com, and employmentdigest. net—and to promote his new podcasts, vlogs, and articles. Bill also uses Twitter to develop new relationships with industry leaders and to research topics for his sites.

For Bill and many other business professionals, Twitter has given him access to hard-to-access professionals and industry leaders. Through Twitter, Bill was able to reach a prominent executive at CBS Careers. Bill, whose background is in recruiting and sourcing, had tried to contact her previously by phone and e-mail without a response. Twitter has allowed Bill to gain access to professionals in a non-obtrusive way, leading to new professional and business connections, increased Web site traffic, and a receptive audience all across the world.

Why Is Twitter a Big Deal?

June 2009

When *Mythbusters* star Adam Savage received an $11,000 bill for cell phone roaming fees from AT&T, Savage chose to communicate his frustration and dissatisfaction with AT&T through the social media platform Twitter. His tweet to his more than 50,000 followers was this, "Text messaging fees are stupid robbery? (they are), AT&T is attempting to charge me 11k for a few hours of Web surfing in Canada. Pls RT!" His message was retweeted by thousands and quickly became the second highest trending topic in a matter of hours just behind the unexpected death of Michael Jackson.

Iran announced their tenth presidential election results with the presidential incumbent, Mahmoud Ahmadinejad, winning by a 63 percent margin against Mir-Hossein Mousavi amongst electoral fraud and police brutality concerns from members of the United Nations. While tensions mounted, Iranian political activists used social media tools, including sites like Twitter, to organize campaigns, communicate, and raise awareness internationally. In Iran, tools such as Twitter have become increasingly important among citizen journalists because news journalists and other international media outlets are restricted from entering the country.

November 2008

While mainstream media struggled to cover the Mumbai attacks, Twitter flexed its muscles and provided a platform for real-time citizen journalism. Every moment of the attacks was documented in harrowing detail on Twitter. Tweets flooded Twitter.com with real-life accounts and pleas for citizens to donate blood. Hundreds of videos of the attacks flooded YouTube and photographer Vinukumar Ranganathan attracted thousands of visits to his Flikr page where he published photos of the attacks. In one tweet, @naomieve said: "Mumbai is not a city under attack as much as it is a social media experiment in action."

All the while, the Indian government pleaded with Twitter users, asking that all updates cease immediately.

Twitter is not just an alternative to SMS text messaging. And from the demographic information listed earlier, you can see that this social media platform is not limited to college students or crazed text-messaging teenagers. Twitter's core audience is highly educated and highly compensated—full of people who are also serious about using Twitter for marketing, publicity, business, and self-promotion. Twitter brings all social media platforms together. Users can post tweets to promote their blog, their newest YouTube video, Flickr updates, and even to cross post their tweets onto Facebook or LinkedIn.

Even if your brand's target market does not fit within Twitter's target demographic, it is important to capture and protect your brand on Twitter before someone else does. This can be accomplished by setting up an account to secure your username, allowing you to protect your online brand without even having to post a picture or send a tweet.

In June 2009, Twitter launched the first phase of its new verified account program. Actors, celebrities, athletes, musicians, public officials, and public agencies on Twitter can now display a "verified account" button on their Twitter pages. Businesses, however, will have to wait until it is offered to corporate entities. Until then, I highly recommend that companies protect and secure their brand by creating a Twitter account even if they have no intent to use the service for marketing or promotional purposes.

Other Social Media Platforms

No one is surprised to know that there are thousands of social media sites and platforms. Here are some of my favorite SM platforms that businesses can use to promote themselves and increase profitability:

Facebook

Founded in 2004 by Harvard student Mark Zuckerberg, Facebook's popularity quickly grew to other Ivy League schools and now boasts over 200 million users worldwide. The service was originally available to students over the age of thirteen, but it has now also gained favor with older generations and professionals. Facebook's popular features among professionals include the events, fan pages, groups, and now, custom URLs. Facebook is banned in some countries such as Iran and Syria.

LinkedIn

LinkedIn was launched in May 2003 and is considered a business networking social media platform. Professional networkers can interact with "connections" online using their network to engage with second- and third-level connections. LinkedIn has over 4 million registered users and offers features that include an online public profile with a custom URL, group features, and forums in which to seek feedback and ask questions.

LinkedIn's basic service is free. They also offer different levels of service that provide members access to more connections, Inmail communication to members they are not connected to, and recruiting and lead generation services.

Ning

Launched in October 2005, Ning offers easy to use, yet customizable, social networking sites free of charge. Those with a computer and as little as ten minutes can create their own custom networking site without purchasing a domain or using HTML or PHP. Because of Ning's ease of use, it is no surprise that these have become very popular as businesses and professionals find ways to differentiate themselves from their competition while engaging customers. Ning reports that they have enabled over 1 million social networks with over 27 million registered users.

MySpace

MySpace launched its site in August 2003 and has been popular among musicians, artists, and photographers as well as high school students. In 2006, MySpace become the most popular social networking site but has recently begun declining in popularity—resulting in a layoff of 30 percent of its workers. MySpace is available in over fifteen languages and almost thirty countries.

YouTube

YouTube—a video sharing Web site—was created by three former PayPal employees in February 2005. Users, both registered and unregistered, can watch videos and embed videos in blogs, other social media platforms, and Web pages. Businesses can use this site to do things such as promote upcoming events, announce job openings, and showcase products and services using video.

SlideShare

SlideShare is the world's largest community for sharing presentations. Organizations and individuals can upload presentations, connect with others, and generate leads for business. Based in San Francisco, California, and New Delhi, SlideShare allows you to upload presentations to be embedded into blogs and Web sites, share your presentation both publicly or privately, market your event or business, and connect with others who have common interests.

Flickr

Flickr is a social media platform that is an image- and video-hosting Web site. As of June 2009, Flickr has more than 3.6 billion images. Launched in February 2004, it is popular with both professional and hobbyist photographers. The site enables subscribers to upload, store, and share photos. Paying users also have the option to upload videos. Flickr has gained increased exposure in light of the Mumbai bombings and Iran election.

Joining the Twitterverse

Understanding the Basics

Creating an account at Twitter.com can be done in less than five minutes. New users can visit the basic Web site at www.Twitter.com and click on the green box at the bottom of the main page that says, "Get Started—Join!" Follow the prompts after reading the entire chapter and you are on your way to "Joining the Twitterverse."

Your Username

The name that you select for your Twitter profile is like a virtual billboard. Customers make quick judgments based on your username and your profile. I urge you to consider the following when creating your username:

- **Brand Consistency**. It is important not to confuse your followers with profiles or usernames that differ from or contradict other social media profiles.

- **Be Creative.** Using a creative Twitter name can grab users' attention and lead them to your Web site or get them engaged in conversation.

- **Stick to it.** Although Twitter allows users the option to change their Twitter name with just a few keystrokes and the click of a mouse, if you choose to change your name, proceed with caution. A name change can cause brand and follower confusion.

Your Profile

As a new user and business professional, it's important to develop credibility—especially when doing so online. Your profile is a way for Twitter users to learn a little more about you, your business, and your talents. Make sure to include your first and last name, information about you, and your area of expertise in your bio. Choose your words carefully—you are limited to 160 characters—and make sure you include industry-related keywords.

In December of 2008, I was listed by recruiter and innovator Jim Stroud, @jimstroud, as one of the fifty top recruiters on Twitter. While I certainly appreciated this honor, the list was generated solely by a keyword search of profile bios on Twitter. Jim's list created a stir in the online recruiting world as recruiters rushed to add other common keywords to their bios. As a result of being listed as one of the top fifty recruiters on Twitter, I gained over two hundred followers.

Another important part of your profile is your Web site address. Your Web site link is a way for businesses and individuals to go beyond 140 characters and learn more about what it is you do. Don't have a Web site? Make sure to include your LinkedIn or Facebook profile address. Many Twitter users—also commonly referred to as "tweeps"—will not follow someone unless they include this information in their profile bio.

Your profile, bio, and even your background are all an essential part of promoting your business and brand on Twitter.

The photo or logo you upload to your Twitter profile is also very important. Users who fail to upload a logo or photo miss an opportunity for the tweeps to connect with you in a visual sense, putting a face to your brand or name. Also keep in mind that photos normally attract more followers than a logo because they add an even more human element to your profile.

Another important part of your profile is your background. Much like your bio, your background can be customized to suit your mood and differentiate you. You can select a background provided by Twitter from your account under *Settings* and then *Design.* This is a great way to differentiate yourself with a colorful background and go beyond 140 characters. Tweeps can also take it a step further by having a custom background created by a designer for a moderate cost or by designing one themselves using Adobe Photoshop. Companies including Twitterbacks. com and Web sites like Designfreebies.org offer free Twitter templates that users can download and use to create their own custom Twitter background. Some of my favorite backgrounds are creative custom backgrounds that take advantage of the additional advertising and promotional space such as those by @koka_sexton, @waynesutton, @ problogger, and many others.

Tweeting

Tweets are short microblog posts written in 140 characters or less on the social media platform Twitter. com. Tweets can include URLs that lead readers to Web pages or other information that answers the question, "What are you doing?"

College Affinity Networking & Social Media including @myworkster
http://is.gd/2224M
9:51 AM Aug 5th from API

Tweeting in 140 characters is an art in itself. Here is one of my tweets that includes a link to a blog post.

How to tweet, what to tweet, and why to tweet depends on you, your business, and the purpose behind engaging the Twitter audience. The key as a business is to have a clear understanding of your goals and what you want to accomplish on Twitter.

Dave Gardner, @fanihiman95376, is a freelance editor located in California. Dave has successfully used LinkedIn to gain freelance editing contracts since December 2007 and joined Twitter in April 2008. Dave, who edits manuscripts in English, Russian, and Japanese, engages other tweeps who have similar likes and interests as well as serving as an expert editor. Dave provides expertise, advice, and free editing samples via Twitter. With over 1,900 followers, Dave has secured multiple editing contracts through his conversations and interactions with other tweeps.

Following vs. Followers

"Following" someone is what you do when you find someone interesting and want to stay up to date by viewing their tweets in your Twitter stream. "Followers" are Twitter users who believe your tweets have value, and they choose to view your tweets among their Twitter stream.

The above example shows a Twitter profile that includes a bio, the number of updates, the number of those followed, and follower count, in addition to Tweets.

There are many ways in which new Twitter users can search and find interesting tweeps to follow. One of the easiest and least complicated ways is from another tweep's profile page under the listing "Following." Profile pictures are displayed in the order in which the Twitter user followed these individuals and businesses from the time they first created their Twitter account until present. Click on an interesting profile picture to view the tweep's profile page, their bio, and a chronological list of their most recent tweets. Select the "Follow" button at the top left side of the tweep's profile page to begin following them. Return to your home page, and the tweets of the users you have chosen to follow are now displayed in your Twitter stream.

Web sites and services you can use to find interesting tweeps to follow include Twittergrader.com, Twellow. com, and Celebritytweet.com. Twittergrader provides services that include the ability to grade your tweets using a special algorithm formula, and it also provides users a list of top tweeps by city in the Twitter Elite Section of the Web site. Celebritytweet.com is a site where you can learn of famous celebrities, sports figures, and political figures who are registered users of Twitter.

Your content is more valuable than follower count. Good content, insightful comments, and a clear and consistent message will organically grow your followers. Do not be fooled into believing that the number of followers determines your celebrity or value on Twitter; having a large number of followers though, does increase the probability that your message will be retweeted or read by others.

I also caution against assuming that following a large number of tweeps will automatically increase your follow account with the idea that everyone will automatically follow you in return.

Just recently, I engaged a Twitter user whose strategy to increase his follower count was by copying and pasting a tweep's bio into a tweet, hoping that the copied tweep would follow him back, thereby increasing his following count. While I don't advocate this method to increase your follower count, it is not uncommon for spammers to use reply tweets in the hopes that the users will automatically follow them and grow their follower count.

When it comes to growing your follower count, I believe in what is called "organic growth." Organic growth is a common business term that translates well into Twitter. Businesses organically grow through traditional methods, including increased sales and output as opposed to acquisitions and mergers. Twitter users can do this in the same way. The key to managing a successful Twitter business account and growing organically is tweeting meaningful content that interests your target audience. What topics grab your audience's attention depends on who your target audience is and how you have gone about reaching them.

At the back of this book is an appendix with worksheets that will help you create your Twitter business strategy. All businesses, whether large or small, must have a business strategy and marketing plan to stay focused and successful. The tools in the appendix will allow you to leverage Twitter and customize your Twitter business strategy to fit your needs.

While completing the questionnaire in the appendix,

ask yourself the following questions when outlining and determining your target market or demographic group you want to reach on Twitter:

- What is the age range of the customer who wants my product or service?
- Which gender would be more interested in this product or service?
- What is the income level of my potential customers?
- What education level do they have?
- What is their marital or family status?
- Is this a product or service they need or is it a luxury item?
- How will they use this product or service?
- What will draw them to this product or service?

Retweeting

As you begin following others and viewing their tweets in your Twitter stream, you may come across a tweet or article you find interesting and useful to others. When this happens, you can retweet, or RT, the post. When doing so, make sure to include the original person's Twitter username and give them credit. You can do this by placing the "@" symbol before the username. The "@" signals to Twitter that a username follows.

If you are using the standard Twitter.com Web site,

RT @hrbartender What are your
thoughts on . . business cards?
http://bit.ly/w4lhS
less than 5 seconds ago from web

Above is an example of a Retweet that includes a shortened URL link.

retweeting is done by cutting and pasting a tweet and reposting the tweet. Third-party Twitter programs such as TweetDeck allow you to retweet a post with the push of a button and without the cutting and pasting. Those who retweet must make sure to include the shorthand for retweet, RT, in the beginning portion of the post while also ensuring that they provide the original Twitter user's credit.

Retweeting is done for the following reasons:

- Reciprocity
- Building relationships
- Product or service recommendation
- Passing along information that you or others may find interesting

At Reply

The "at reply" is a way to speak directly to one user at a virtual cocktail party. You must place the "@" symbol before the user's Twitter name like this: "@SoonerExecRec." Intended users can view their @replies by selecting this option on their Twitter page. One caution: @replies are not private conversations between Twitter users. These conversations are visible to anyone in the Twitter stream and also on your profile.

Direct Messaging

Direct messaging is a way to have a private conversation between two Twitter users in 140 characters or less via Twitter. Only the messenger and recipient can view and read the direct message. *Both users must be following one another to be able to send a direct message, also known as a DM.*

Direct Messages are a way to contact Twitter users privately while @Replies allow your message to be viewed by everyone in the Twitter stream.

Another benefit to using a direct message as opposed to an @reply is that most tweeps set up direct messages to be directly forwarded to their cell phones or e-mail. This is an easy way to get someone's attention almost immediately, since most Twitter users are extremely tech savvy and technically connected (especially with the popularity of smart phones like the BlackBerry Bold and iPhone).

Your Privacy

Be advised though that Twitter accounts—unless protected—are public. If someone you work with from your company tweets information that could be considered suspect or unprofessional, you might consider recommending your employees curtail their risqué content. Another alternative is to ask employees to create two Twitter accounts—one for business and one for pleasure. To learn more about legal considerations specifically surrounding privacy, turn to Chapter Seven: Legal Considerations.

Basic Twitter Applications

For a new user, Twitter and the user's tweet stream can be viewed using the basic www.twitter.com Web site. Because the Twitter platform is written in open code, developers can create applications to compliment Twitter—allowing users increased features. Hundreds of Twitter applications are created and added daily. Listed below are some popular third-party, or API, applications that make using Twitter easier.

Twitter Search

This Web site is a way to use Twitter as a real-time search engine like Google and is searchable by keyword topic. Use the advanced search options and refine your search by zip code, date, or by users. This application also allows users to sign up for RSS feeds using a site like iGoogle and organize tweets containing keywords of your choosing. Visitors to the site can see trending topics that are on the minds and thoughts of tweeps.

> NOW I'm burning the midnight oil. And I'm about to rob Peter to pay Paul. #zzzz #upbeforedawntofinishtheproject
> 12:36 AM Jul 27th from web

An example of hash tag humor by Sheri Guyse, @myjrny.

On June 25, 2009, while the world held its breath for news concerning the health of Michael Jackson and his reported cardiac arrest, Twitter exploded with the phrase "Michael Jackson" for almost 30 percent of all tweets. While on my couch with my eyes glued to Search.Twitter. com, I watched as thousands of Twitter posts containing the keyword phrase "Michael Jackson" updated every two to three seconds.

Twitter Search allows you to search by what is referred to as a "hashtag." A hashtag is a community-driven convention for adding additional context to your tweets. Think of them like tags for your blog and Flickr pages with the difference being only that Twitter users add the hashtag to their posts. You create a hashtag simply by prefixing a word with a hash symbol: *#hashtag*. Hashtags were created as a way to create groups on Twitter. Anyone can create a hashtag and use it to sort for groups. Some common hashtags include #followfriday, #jobs, #quote, and #iphone.

Hashtags are also a common way to emphasize a tweet's intended purpose specifically for a joke or humor.

TweetDeck

TweetDeck offers custom options for each individual user including customized groups, keyword search, and follow your stocks.

TweetDeck is a downloadable software Twitter application for use on desktops and is compatible with Mac or Microsoft Windows. According to TwitStat, it is the most popular Twitter desktop application. TweetDeck enables you to create groupings, perform keyword searches, and manage your tweets, DM's, and @replies without toggling or refreshing your screens. TweetDeck notifies you each time it updates with a short beep, enabling you to multitask while managing your account simultaneously.

TweetDeck also offers an iPhone application that allows users to create groups on their desktop account and integrate it to their iPhone.

SocialOomph

One of my favorite Twitter applications, SocialOomph, is an application that allows registered users to schedule their tweets, shorten URLs, and create autofollows, keyword alerts, automatic messages, and more on the Web site, www.SocialOomph.com.

Autofollows allow you to automatically follow someone that begins to follow you. Users can send automatic or canned messages via direct message to new followers. The basic SocialOomph application is free. SocialOomph also offers a professional level of service for a fee. Other similar sites such as Hootsuite, Britekite, and Twittertise offer similar services. One of the benefits of these others is that they display the number of click-through links that you insert into a tweet. This is helpful if you are interested in seeing how many tweeps clicked on your link and viewed the blog post or URL you posted using their service.

I advise caution when making the decision to use sites like SocialOomph to auto-follow or auto-DM new followers. Users who chose the above mentioned are often labeled spammers, and some tweeps will automatically unfollow users who send self-publicizing DMs. Auto-DMs are like any business decision—leaders must weigh the pros and cons when choosing to make a decision to promote their brand, product, or service.

Tweetvisor

Tweetvisor is an Internet-based Twitter application that offers services similar to TweetDeck. Some of Tweetvisor's features include the ability to create groups, RSS keywords, and allowing Twitter users easy access in viewing @replies and direct messages sorted by columns. Tweetvisor is similar to TweetDeck in that it offers the above services except that users can manage their Twitter accounts from the Web versus downloading a desktop application.

Twellow

Twellow.com enables users to cut through the clutter and allow them to search for users by industry—thus allowing the Twellow visitor to connect with others with greater ease. I use Twellow to search for tweeps to follow by industry and location—it has been helpful when looking for nearby businesses like florists and coffee shops.

Use Twellow to follow those that interest you by keyword search or category.

recommend that you register for Twellow. The process is relatively simple—your Twellow profile displays your Twitter bio and profile picture along with a handful of recent tweets and the industries or business categories your company is associated with. Users can provide their contact information including their phone number and e-mail address in addition to an extended bio in two thousand words or less, a novel by Twitter standards.

Bit.ly

Bit.ly is a Web site that enables users to shorten the length of a URL and then track the resulting usage. Bit.ly can be used for Twitter as well as any other Web site. One of the advantages to Bit.ly versus SocialOomph is that there is no need to register and you can track URL clicks. Users provide their Twitter username and password on Bit.ly and post their tweets with shortened URLs directly from the site.

Bit.ly boasts a Firefox plug-in that enables users to hover their mouse over the Twitter link and see the page and link details before clicking.

Twitter Grader

Twitter Grader (www.twittergrader.com) allows Twitter users to enter their screen names (and the names of others) into its "secret algorithmic stuff" generator and find out how each user ranks on the Twitter scale. Twitter Grader grades uses by taking the following into account:

- Number of followers
- Number of followers that your followers have
- Quantity and pace of updates
- Additional proprietary analysis

This application also allows you to search top Twitter users by location and provides other interesting applications, including TwitSnip and Tweetit.

TweetBeep

TweetBeep provides e-mail updates to registered users based on keywords from Twitter posts. Users can choose keywords, zip code radius, and the duration at which they receive the e-mail updates. TweetBeep is a great option for receiving updates on commonly misspelled words or services that relate to your business. My personal TweetBeep account includes the keyword "bloggingforjobs," which is slightly different than my Twitter username, @blogging4jobs. I receive e-mail updates from TweetBeep if the keyword "bloggingforjobs" is mentioned in any tweets. Businesses can use this service as a way to manage their brand in real time without hitting the refresh on sites like Search.Twitter every fifteen seconds.

Twitscoop

Twitscoop is another fully featured Twitter client in that it enables you to sign in with your Twitter username and password and post and follow tweets. The service has a mesmerizing quality as it automatically updates trending Twitter topics; the bigger and more bold the keyword, the more hot the topic. Currently, Gmail, Coke, and Porch are hot topics.

Twitpic

Twitpic is a third-party application that allows tweeps to share pictures on Twitter. Twitpics can be sent from a phone or a PC on Twitter using a URL that when clicked displays your picture. Visitors to Twitpic can leave photo comments or post their own photos after creating an account at www.twitpic.com.

Twitter for the Traveler

Social media platforms like Twitter have made the world smaller, literally allowing for millions of clients, customers, and contacts at our fingertips. Mobile technologies like iPhones, BlackBerries, and text messaging have made staying connected and reaching new audiences from a business perspective easier and more convenient.

Twitter users can change their account setting to stay connected through Twitter's SMS text messaging features.

This allows users without mobile Internet access to receive text messages alerting users to a new direct message. Under the settings heading and devices option, users can adjust their setting features by first turning on their mobile phone device updates to connect to Twitter directly by text. Directly post tweets to your Twitter account by texting updates to 40404. After setting up the mobile device option, users can request to receive texts when receiving direct messages and e-mail notifications when someone starts following them under the notices heading.

iPhones are one of the best ways to stay connected anywhere using downloadable Twitter applications. Just like desktop applications, iPhone Twitter applications offer a wide variety by price and features. Just like selecting a third-party Twitter application, it's important to do your research. Visit blogs and Web sites for reviews and ratings. Listed below are a handful of some of the most common and popular iPhone Twitter applications with business specifically in mind.

Tweetie

A popular iPhone Twitter application, Tweetie enables users to manage multiple Twitter accounts from their iPhone. Tweetie can be downloaded from iTunes at a cost of $2.99 and includes keyword search features, the ability to post photos using Twitpic, and the ability to easily designate tweets as favorites. When designating a tweet as a favorite, it is listed with a gold star. People can view your profile, read your bio, and view the posts you have flagged as a favorite. I use the "favorite" flag as a way to group tweets or blog posts I am interested in reading at some other time when I am less busy. Tweeps can view their own designated favorites from their Twitter.com home page by selecting the Favorites link just below the @reply link on the right side.

TwitterFon

Available free and downloadable from iTunes, TwitterFon is another Twitter application for use with the iPhone. TwitterFon is easy to use. Users can tweet, @ reply, direct message, see favorites, upload photos, and track trending topics much like Tweetie. Unlike Tweetie, TwitterFon users cannot toggle multiple Twitter accounts or search for keywords or Twitter users. TwitterFon is a great Twitter application for a first-time iPhone user or someone who only manages one Twitter account.

TweetDeck

TweetDeck Mobile syncs directly with the third-party desktop TweetDeck option. This iPhone application provides users the ability to seamlessly transition group lists from desktop to mobile device. Free to iPhone users, TweetDeck Mobile offers the ability to manage multiple accounts, share photos and links, and search Twitter.

Twitter for Business

Companies Who Converse

Twitter is about developing relationships, branding your business, solidifying relationships through real-time customer engagement, and marketing your business to new and different audiences. Twitter should be about putting your company out there and communicating with potential clients, customers, and your competition.

Some companies are well-known for great interaction with their customers using Twitter.

- @JetBlue and @comcastcares use Twitter for customer service. JetBlue customers can visit the @JetBlue Twitter profile to learn about flight delays and instantly receive answers to specific questions about rebooking flights or changing seats. @

comcastcares is managed by Frank Eliason, the director of Digital Care. Eliason discovered during an Internet search using the term "Comcast" that he could connect with tweeps and provide immediate customer service solutions. His team answers technical questions and directs customers to their e-mail for more assistance. Some of Comcast's customer support staff have their own separate Twitter accounts to engage multiple customers instantaneously.

JetBlue uses Twitter to notify travelers of weather and cancelations.

- The @thehomedepot Twitter account is managed by Sarah. She tweets about Home Depot's sales and specials, answers questions, and helps promote Home Depot in the news, including employees' outside-of-work stories and other interesting articles.

- @zappos' Twitter account is managed by CEO Tony Hsieh and has helped humanize and promote the Zappos brand. Unlike many other CEOs who use ghostwriters to manage their accounts, Tony manages his own Twitter account and posts tweets regularly about his travels and engages customers and fans. Many other CEOs and executives have followed suit in response to the positive publicity and media coverage Hsieh has received.

Tony Hsieh is one of the first CEOs to use Twitter as a way to promote his company, Zappos.

Professionals Who Tweet

Professionals from companies both large and small are finding success using Twitter to promote themselves, build credibility, network with other professionals, and drive traffic to their business.

Becky McCray, @BeckyMccray, first joined Twitter in 2006 after being encouraged by friend, Chris Brogan, @chrisbrogan. Becky has enjoyed watching Twitter evolve from a service that connects family and friends with already established relationships to a platform where people forge new connections and promote their businesses—sharing and challenging the future of the way businesses connect. Becky, a small-business owner, entrepreneur, and publisher, uses Twitter to network with other professionals and drive traffic to her Web site www. smallbizsurvival.com.

Another Oklahoma tweep is Matt Galloway, @ mattgalloway. Matt's analytical and data-gathering expertise is helping bring to light trends and best practices for Twitter users all across the country. Matt's Web site, www.thebasement.com, provides information on the data-driven side of Twitter. His passion for the back-side of Twitter is especially beneficial for professionals like me who often tweet now and evaluate later. One of his more recent projects researches Twitter trends specifically related to registered Twitter users from Oklahoma.

In January 2009, Mark Stelzner, @stelzner—a human resource consultant—was sitting at home enjoying his breakfast and contemplating the current economic and unemployment crisis. He had a thought that led to a tweet—"Was thinking that if each of us helped just one person find a job, we could start making a dent in unemployment. You game?" This one tweet led to a non-profit company, called Job Angels. Job Angels' mission is helping people find employment using social media.

Volunteers manage every part of the business from the LinkedIn group and Twitter to the Facebook fan page. @JobAngels uses Twitter as a way to engage its audience in real-time, seeking out others to help those in need of finding employment. To date, over 500,000 messages have been sent from Job Angels.

What to Tweet

During my Twitter training seminars, I recommend to those new to Twitter that instead of answering the question, "What are you doing?" you answer the question, "What has your attention?" This opens up possibilities of topics to tweet and starts a dialogue between you and your followers. What is important to remember about Twitter is that in order to get, you must give. Giving can be accomplished through quotes, posting links to articles or Web sites that interest you, and retweeting.

It is also important to tweet about others and those who you follow and are interested in. Developing relationships and growing followers takes time and preparation, and it involves interacting with others.

Use Twitter to ask questions. Twitter is great for getting opinions and real-time answers. I have used Twitter to get recommendations on restaurants and coffee shops when travelling and also for finding more obscure things like a creative memory consultant and a Mariachi band. One of the great things about Twitter is that it attracts users from all over the world, so your opinions and recommendations from others will be quite different and varied—especially depending upon the day and time during which you choose to tweet.

Samuel Gordons Jewelers is a third-generation family jewelry company founded over a hundred years ago. Daniel Gordon, the forth generation of Samuel Gordons, ,manages the company's social media, including their Facebook and Twitter accounts. Daniel is very passionate about his family's company and about putting people first in everything Samuel Gordons does.

Daniel's first priority online was to develop his personal online brand: @DanGordon. Next, he worked at developing the company's brand: @SamuelGordons; and he believes sales will follow. Although Samuel Gordons has been a member of Twitter for almost two years, Daniel admits that he didn't get Twitter at first and logged onto the site again a little over a year ago.

In July 2009, a customer @replied @DanGordon on a Saturday to tell him that he was coming by the store with someone he wanted Daniel to meet. Although the two had never met face to face, they followed each other via Twitter. Later that afternoon, the customer left the store a satisfied customer, and Daniel's online strategy resulted in an $8,000 sale.

I also recommend that you give advice and opinions about interesting topics that are newsworthy. Many tweeps follow users solely based on trending topics and keywords used within tweets. Don't forget to share the human side of your story. People want to get to know the person behind the tweets. Follow the Social Media Mullet Rule by leading with your business tweets, keeping them in the forefront, and leaving your "party," or personal tweets, in the background.

As a business and Twitter account user, you walk a fine line between promoting yourself and your business and becoming Twitter spam. According to Twitter's support page, spam can be considered the following:

- Following a large number of users in a short amount of time as well as following and unfollowing large numbers repeatedly.
- Having a small number of followers compared to the amount of people you are following.
- Your updates consist mainly of links and not personal updates.
- A large number of spam complaints have been filed against you using @spam.
- Posting multiple duplicate posts on one account or multiple accounts.
- Selling your account or followers to others.

Be advised that although the account contains your

original content, Twitter does own the rights to your account and can terminate your account without notice at any time. If your account does become suspended or you have technical difficulties with your account, users can complete an online form and receive a ticket request number. Twitter promises to respond within thirty days; which, in Web 2.0, is several lifetimes. There is no 1-800 number to contact them directly.

Proceed with caution when posting on Twitter and following a large number of tweeps quickly. Growing your Twitter followers organically is important and takes time. I received a frantic phone call from a professional contact who had been suspended by Twitter for suspicious activity. After a series of questions, we determined that she had provided her Twitter account information and password to a third-party site and was suspended because the third-party site was spamming her followers using her account. She submitted a ticket request and within a week, her account was back up and running. Although hard, she learned two very valuable lessons concerning social media: (1) the importance of growing your follower count organically, and (2) do not provide outside applications with your Twitter account information and password.

Most importantly, be yourself both offline and online. Successful users of Twitter can develop online relationships while using the tool to further strengthen their offline relationships. Part of staying true to your brand plan is being consistent with one voice.

Chef Ryan Parrott does an excellent job of using Twitter as a way to generate new business and develop and nurture relationships. Parrott, known as @chefrp on Twitter, owns a successful catering company called Season's Catering and two restaurants, Table One and Iguana Mexican Grill. Parrott's businesses were launched In July 2008, and his Twitter account soon followed in October. Parrott has two separate Twitter accounts, @chefrp and @Table1okc. His Table One restaurant is just as it sounds; one table with a full commercial kitchen where he cooks specialty dinners for groups of eight or more. Parrott says that he has booked over twenty dinner reservations, several catering contracts, and other specialty events using Twitter. What distinguishes Parrott from other business Twitter users is that he does not use Twitter as an advertising tool but primarily as a way to allow others to get to know him as a person. Parrott says, "Twitter is like a television commercial. People can choose who they read and who they don't."

Following Others

From your Twitter account, you may follow everyone you know who uses Twitter. Follow colleagues in related companies and throughout your industry. Follow relevant brands, journalists, and pundits in your market. Follow even those who compete against you. By following those who interest you, you are creating an ecosystem in which business people will see whom you are following and consider those as suggestions for whom they should follow as well.

Trichology Salon, @Trichology, joined Twitter in February 2009. Trichology is a technology-based salon that offers hair cuts, color, makeup, and waxing services in a cool and modern atmosphere. Their salon, located in Oklahoma City, offers clients online booking services, a coffee bar, and wireless Internet. With the high style and technology that differentiates Trichology from the other salons in the Oklahoma City Metro area, it was a natural step for them to join Twitter. @Trichology has 1,050 followers and uses Twitter as a way for customers to inquire about offered services and available appointment times. Trichology also uses Twitter to promote their salon, posting frequent before and after pictures to showcase their work.

Greg Welchel, the creative genius behind Trichology is quick to admit that when it comes to social media and Twitter he has learned some hard lessons along the way. Greg encourages his stylists to manage their own separate Twitter accounts while Greg manages @gwelchel and @Trichology. This allows his team to engage a variety of different demographics and customers at the same time while the @Trichology account has a consistent voice and message.

Early on, Welchel says the @Trichology account was flagged as spam and suspended after an assistant followed over 1,500 tweeps in under one day. Because Trichology is a local salon, Welchel says he follows mostly local accounts and those that are industry related.

Oftentimes when following someone, you will immediately receive an e-mail notification that this tweep reciprocates and follows you back. This is called an auto-follow. Third-party programs discussed earlier can be used to compliment Twitter.com and programmed to auto-follow as well as auto-direct message.

Recommend Others to Tweet

People use Twitter for a thousand different reasons and in a thousand different ways. Not everyone you know will embrace Twitter, but many will follow your lead. Twitter can help you make stronger personal connections with those you already have an established relationship or connection with.

I recommend not just setting up one company account from which to tweet. If you have employees, partners, or others you work with, encourage them to tweet as part of your company's marketing and branding plan.

Multiple posts coming from different Twitter accounts about an upcoming event or a new or interesting product will reach more followers and individuals from different demographics, businesses, and customer segments than just one Twitter account alone. The *Oklahoma Gazette,* an Oklahoma social publication, encourages its employees to do this very thing, and it has worked well for promoting many of their upcoming issues and events. One of their most successful events was the Oklahoma Social Rave in March 2009. The Oklahoma Social Rave was a flash event promoted solely through Twitter. Suspense was built throughout the Oklahoma City Metro tweeps who waited in anticipation to learn about the location of the social rave just thirty minutes before the event began, using the hashtag #oksocialrave. For its creators, @okgazette, @chefrp, and @COOPAleWorks the social rave resulted in over 130 in attendance and also brought increased media relations to the businesses involved both on a local and national level. The hashtag #oksocialrave also became one of the top ten trending topics for the day.

Instant Real-Time Search Engine

Use Web sites such as Search.Twitter.com to monitor posts containing mention of your company or industry information pertaining to you. This enables you to immediately engage an unhappy customer, quickly limiting the negative publicity and impact.

Below, I have used Search.Twitter.com to search for Twitter posts that include the keywords "car repair." By using Twitter as a search engine, you can view real-time results of users mentioning the keywords "car repair" in their tweets, and I can directly engage these potential customers, offering them my company's services. Search. Twitter.com also provides an advanced search feature that

tfaust: Need an **oil change** in Iowa. I had forgotten that in Real America, everything is closed on Sunday.
36 minutes ago from *txt* · Reply · View Tweet

Use Twitter Search for real-time search results to expand your business and engage a customer in real time.

can narrow the search by specifics like zip code.

Brand Recognition & Management

In addition to using Twitter as a real-time search engine and a place to communicate, Twitter, along with other social media platforms, can be used to promote your brand and develop brand recognition through a "Brand Plan." This is important as your tweets and their content can aid in developing your online brand and reputation either positively or negatively.

Just like a marketing plan, your Brand Plan will vary depending on your overall business or personal branding goal. Brand plans have been effective in developing customer loyalty, culture, product differentiation, and competitive advantage. A well-thought-out Brand Plan can be the deciding factor in delivering a consistent brand and message on not only Twitter but all different social media platforms. It's important to step back and consider your brand's voice, colors, information, and textures for your profile as your signature theme that separates you from your competition and others within your industry. Your Brand Plan will help you define this. As a recruiter, my Brand Plan seeks to provide tips and tricks on the job hunt and help others to learn the unwritten rules of the job search. I also provide my audience with a daily Job Search Tip in addition to new blog posts from my peers or myself.

Job seekers can use Twitter as a method of differentiation and competitive advantage. Eddie Roach, @eddieroach, joined Twitter in October 2008 and was laid off from his position in Marketing and Sales with a technology company in early 2009. Eddie used multiple social media platforms as well as phone and e-mail communication to notify his network of personal and professional contacts. @eddieroach, who had just seventy-five updates and 160 followers, sent a post on June 5, 2009, notifying his followers he would be offline for a week on vacation. Almost immediately, Eddie was contacted by a follower from Twitter about an open position at a former employer.

Eddie quickly applied before heading out of state. And just seventeen days later, Eddie's tweet announced to his audience his first day at his new position.

Whole Foods uses Twitter in a variety of ways and with great success. Their corporate Twitter account has over 1 million followers.

One company that does an excellent job of brand recognition and management is Whole Foods. Whole Foods uses Twitter for various things including monitoring customer questions and feedback, driving traffic to their blog, and promotion of new products. Whole Foods encourages each individual store location to create and manage their own Twitter account to promote events and specials specific to their geographic location.

In May 2009, Revolution Magazine published information that revealed the top 100 most mentioned brands on Twitter over a three-day period in April 2009. Not surprisingly, the most mentioned brand was Starbucks with 3.37 million mentions; yes, million. Google followed as number 2 with 1.01 million, then came the BBC with 703,000 mentions, and Apple with 512,000. Finishing the top 5 was AIG with 455,000 mentions.

Shockingly enough, out of the top five listed, only Starbucks, Google, and the BBC actually have Twitter accounts. What Revolution Magazine's article also exposes is that not every post or mention of a brand is always positive. AIG is a glaring example. AIG's name and brand is associated with the most recent economic recession, wasteful corporate spending, and the housing and financial crisis in the United States and throughout the rest of the world. Part of your business and marketing strategy both online and off should include an emergency and damage control marketing plan. During times like these, an effective damage control plan, along with seasoned public relations or communications professionals, can prove invaluable. It's important to understand that by engaging your business on social media platforms such as Twitter, you can quickly react to negative comments, evaluate trends, and also develop defensive marketing strategies to handle less-than-stellar reviews or articles before they go viral.

Use Twitter to Ask Questions

Use Twitter to engage customers in real time and get real answers. Starbucks uses Twitter as a way to promote their new line of instant coffees by offering a free sample for Twitter users—driving them to the Starbucks company Web site for the coupon. Once customers received the free samples, they provided Starbucks with real customer feedback in real time using Twitter.

Comcast uses Twitter to answer customer questions and provide technical support.

Twitter Tips

Mullet Media Golden Rule

Businesses, professionals, and entrepreneurs who are new to Twitter often struggle with the balance between business tweets and professional ones. On the one hand, it's important to stay focused on promoting your company and managing your brand. And on the other, it's important to show your market the human and personal side that customers and followers can relate with.

I recommend to new business Twitter users that, just like the popular '80s hairstyle the mullet, our tweets should follow what I call the Social Media Mullet Rule: "Business in the front and party in the back." Basically, keep most of your tweets professional and related to your business, roughly 70 percent of all tweets. The remaining 30 percent of your tweets should be personal while still allowing the reader to see your true authentic self. This allows your followers to see past the logo or marketing propaganda and find a commonality or interest that can solidify the business relationship or customer experience.

Post Often and with Meaningful Content

To engage your Twitter audience, make an effort to tweet regularly with meaningful content. Tweet about subjects that your readers might be interested in, solicit their feedback, and engage in conversation. Five to ten business-related tweets a day is a good, solid number in which to engage your audience while not appearing to be overly spammy or selfishly business driven. Work hard to post comments and information that can relate to your target audience and that creates interesting and thought-provoking conversations to have people talking offline with others, promoting your brand.

Sharlyn Lauby, known to the Twitterverse as @hrbartender is a business owner and human resource consultant for her company, Internal Talent Management, located in South Florida. Lauby's @hrbartender account boasts over 2,800 followers. Lauby uses Twitter to connect with people and promote herself and her company's services as well as her award-winning blog, www.hrbartender.

com. Although she has never secured a consulting contract as a direct result of Twitter, Lauby has secured a number of professional speaking engagements that resulted in several assignments. Lauby has multiple Twitter accounts, including @hrbartender and @sharlyn_lauby, and also uses FeedFriend, LinkedIn, and Facebook accounts to further market and solidify relationships while driving traffic to her Web site.

THE HR BARTENDER

I'm Sharlyn Lauby - the HR Bartender. And, yes, I am an expert with more than 18 years of professional HR management experience. Over the years, I found that my colleagues and employees wanted me to be like their neighborhood bartender - that friendly face who's there when you need them. **Click to learn more . . .**

Sharlyn Lauby known as the @hrbartender on Twitter uses Twitter to drive traffic to her blog and position herself as an expert in her field.

With both accounts, Lauby does a phenomenal job of engaging others and posting content that her target audience can relate to. As the HR Bartender, she provides workplace tips and advice in a candid and professional yet approachable way with a good mix of comments, @replies, and self-marketing and promotion.

Retweeting as a Form of Flattery

Want to stay in the good graces of those you follow when you find something interesting while viewing your Twitter stream? Retweeting is the best way to do both and is an essential part of managing a successful Twitter account to promote your business. When retweeting, it is extremely important to give tweeps credit for their tweets.

I often retweet someone as a jumping-off point to start a conversation with that person whom I admire and want to develop an off-line relationship with.

Retweeting is a way to virtually say, "I love that purse," or, "Your article on small business strategies got my attention." I have not met anyone who doesn't appreciate a positive comment or recognition for their hard work.

Offline Twitter Conversation

Some conversations between tweeps need more than 140 characters. Ask to engage the user offline either by phone, e-mail, or even Skype. This is a great way to take Twitter networking to the next level, building on the relationship. For me, Twitter has been a great way to make connections with people from all across the world.

If you are a blogger, asking to interview a tweep is a great way to develop an offline relationship as well as a link exchange. Invite followers and new connections to network with you on other social media platforms like

Facebook, Plaxo, and LinkedIn. Do not be afraid to meet other tweeps face-to-face over coffee or a Tweetup, also known as a Twitter Meetup. Face-to-face interaction is a great way to grow personal relationships.

6

Twitter Resources

The Twitter community is full of great information about a variety of topics including Twitter and social media marketing. Below are some Web sites, blogs, and tweets I recommend you visit and follow regularly:

Blogs and Web Sites

- **Mashable:** (http://Mashable.com). Mashable is a social media guide that discusses all things about social media. The site, managed by Pete Cashmore, was founded in 2005 and has over 6 million monthly page views. Pete and his team offer social media resources, lists, guides, and other resources on social media for social media enthusiasts.

- **TwiTips Blog:** (www.twitip.com). Darren Rowse currently authors several blogs and is one of the first bloggers to make blogging a full-time career. He provides great insight into the world of blogging and social media. Relatively new to Twitter, he provides creative ways to use this new social media platform.

Darren Rowse, known as @problogger on Twitter, is one of the first bloggers to make blogging a full-time career.

- **Mari Smith**: (www.marismith.com). Mari Smith is a relationship marketing specialist and social media business coach. She is passionate about showing fellow professionals how to develop powerful and profitable relationships using social media. Her site discusses ways to strengthen both online and offline relationships to drive sales and your business.

- **Chris Brogan Marketing Blog:** (www.chrisbrogan. com). Chris is known worldwide for his use of social media and creative marketing strategies. He is the president of New Marketing Labs and works with small to large companies to improve online business communications like marketing and PR. Chris is known for pushing the envelope and blazing new trails in the social media industry.

- **Twitter Blog:** (http://blog.twitter.com). This blog is managed by Twitter and provides readers with Twitter support and updates.

- **SlideShare:** (www.slideshare.net). SlideShare is a presentation hosting and social media site that is similar to YouTube but enables its users to upload, share, and display Powerpoint presentations to anyone who has access to the World Wide Web.

Recommended Tweeps to Follow

- @blogging4jobs. This is my Twitter name. I enjoy helping businesses and professionals know how to use social media platforms like Twitter to grow their business and find employment.

- @chrisbrogan. I mentioned Chris earlier. He is one of the revolutionaries in driving the way businesses use and leverage social media.

- @MarketingTwins. Randy Vaughn is a business coach and marketer. His and his brother's site, www.marketingtwins.com, discusses new trends and ways for businesses to market themselves or their products using social media. Randy is Ft. Worth's only Duct Tape Marketing Coach.

- @problogger. I mentioned Darren earlier in this book as well. He has multiple Twitter accounts including @digitalps. In addition to www.problogger. net, Darren has a digital photography Web site at http://digital-photography-school.com/.

- @waynesutton. Wayne Sutton lives in Raleigh, North Carolina, and is responsible for the successful Triangle Tweetup. Known as "Social Wayne," he provides social media strategy, consulting, and coaching.

- @giovanni. Giovanni Gallucci is known for Wordcamp, a Wordpress camp for bloggers and programmers. He provides social media and interactive marketing services through Simply Interactive.

- @MariSmith. Mari Smith was named the Pied Piper of the online world by fastcompany.com. Her tweets and blog provide insight into using platforms like Twitter and social media as a way to grow sales and accelerate business profits.

- @mashable. Pete Cashmore's site, http://mashable.com, provides breaking news and insight into all aspects of social media. His site is a great resource for social media enthusiasts from beginners to the more advanced users.

- @danschawbel. Dan Schawbel is a leading personal branding expert for Generation Y and a social media specialist. Dan's insightful articles and blog posts are worth a second and third look.

- @jeffpulver. Jeff Pulver is a technological anthropologist and founder of the 140 Conference that brought social media experts and innovators from all across the world together to discuss the future of social media. I recommend visiting his blog at www.jeffpulver.com.

- @koka_sexton. Koka Sexton's Web site's tagline is "just another geek with a blog." Koka calls himself a geek with a mind for business. An admitted Twitter addict, his site, www.kokasexton.com, is full of great information for creative business and innovation.

- @murnahan. Mark Aaron Murnahan helps businesses increase their market share. His site, www.awebguy.com, provides search engine optimization (SEO) tips and strategies through his company YourNew.com Inc. His blog provides an original and distinct voice.

Legal Considerations

Generally speaking, laws and court decisions are created and tested after the fact. For the legal world, social media is in its infancy. It's important to understand that just because there is not a law that specifically addresses social media this doesn't give users a free ticket to tweet without consciousness. The legal and court systems use past case history and law to apply to the new world of social media. Educate yourself about possible legal considerations and formulate your social media strategy accordingly. I recommend you contact an attorney for professional guidance when factoring in legal considerations as part of your Brand Plan.

Latoicha Givens, a practicing attorney with more than ten years' experience and a managing partner with Phillips

Givens, LLC, specializes in intellectual property issues, trademarks, domain names, copyrights, licensing, and legal issues in new media. Givens encourages Twitter users to read Twitter's terms of service agreement in its entirety before creating a new account. With any marketing and brand strategy, businesses and professionals need to take into consideration the risks associated when representing your brand. Businesses walk a fine line when choosing to engage an audience on social media. Understanding social media and its positive or negative implications are of the utmost importance.

One case study example with negative brand implications is a libel lawsuit filed by Horizon Group Management, LLC, in July 2009 against Twitter user Amanda Bonnen, @abonnen. Horizon Group Management, LLC, is located in Chicago, Illinois, and alleges that a tweet posted by @abonnen maliciously and wrongfully damaged Horizon's reputation. The tweet, posted on May 12, 2009, reads in part, "Who said sleeping in a moldy apartment was bad for you? Horizon really thinks it's okay." After filing the suit, Horizon, which is seeking $50,000 in damages was thrust into the national spotlight—the *Chicago-Sun Times,* bloggers, and the Associated Press picked up the story.

Twitter Terms of Service

Like any social networking platform, Twitter has a terms of service agreement, outlined in detail at http://twitter.com/tos. By using the Twitter.com site, you as the user are agreeing to be bound by their Terms and Conditions.

Some highlights and points to consider concerning Twitter's terms of service:

- You are responsible for activity under your screen name.

- You must not abuse, threaten, impersonate, or intimidate other Twitter users.

- You must not create or submit unwanted e-mails to any Twitter members (spam).

- Twitter specifically provides its users with a detailed section discussing copyright. They claim no intellectual rights over the material you provide to Twitter.

- Twitter will also remove content that is unlawful, offensive, threatening, libelous, defamatory, obscene, or objectionable.

- Twitter prohibits the unauthorized use of another's trademark. If you use another's trademark without their permission, the owner can contact Twitter and request that the unauthorized account is deleted.

Copyright

It is not uncommon for me to see tweets in my Twitter stream that include a quote or hashtag designation as part of a conference or live tweeting event. Live tweeting as well as live blogging during events and conferences have given rise to concerns surrounding copyright. The Fair Use provision of U.S. copyright law, allows a certain percentage of a copyrighted work to be reproduced for purposes such as a review of a book or theatrical play. On its Web site, the U.S. Copyright Office outlines factors that affect whether reproduction of a copyrighted work is considered fair use:

- "The purpose and character of the use, including whether such use is of commercial nature or is for nonprofit educational purposes
- The nature of the copyrighted work
- The amount and substantiality of the portion used in relation to the copyrighted work as a whole
- The effect of the use upon the potential market for, or value of, the copyrighted work"

As you can see, the distinction between fair use and infringement is often unclear and not easily defined. There is no specific number of words, lines, or notes that may safely be taken without permission, and even tweets could be considered a copyright violation.

Fair use is in the eyes of the beholder, and according

to Social Media Today, the government will not rule on what is or isn't fair use, leaving it to the judgment of the individual, and in some cases, the courts to make the ultimate determination.

A practical approach is to place yourself in the author or creator's shoes and ask, "Does the speaker or writer intend for this information to be free of charge?" The backbone of social media and Web 2.0 is the right and ability to freely share, distribute, and reproduce ideas, thoughts, and information to others quickly using a multitude of channels. Certainly, it is important to give the creator or originator credit which can certainly be challenging when limited to 140 characters. I recommend using a third-party application like Twitlonger, which allows you to use more than 140 characters. Twitlonger creates a URL link which tweeps can click on to see the full content of your tweet.

The Twitter Support Resources site at http://help. twitter.com provides Twitter users information about Twitter's terms of service and the process for filing a complaint through e-mail at copyright@twitter.com.

Defamation & Privacy

Companies may face liability if their employees post content to a company-represented or affiliated Twitter account that defames or invades the privacy of third parties. Posts that include a third party's intellectual property may be held as libelous.

An example of this is the recent defamation case filed against Courtney Love. Courtney is being sued for making an alleged defamatory tweet about a famous fashion designer, Dawn Simorangkir. A defamatory statement is spoken or written words that are false and/or misleading that gives the defamed a negative image or hurts their reputation. Because Twitter is generally in written form, libel is the most common form of defamation. The spoken form of defamation, called slander, is more common on social media platforms like YouTube or other Web 2.0 voice applications. However, URL links posted on Twitter leading to defamatory videos could pose a slander risk.

Givens stated on her blog, www.iplaw101.com, on June 23, 2009, "Under the Communications Decency Act, an owner of a social networking site is not liable for the defamatory statements made about another on their site unless the site owner actively engages in the gathering of information from the user that leads to the defamatory statement." Ms. Givens further states, "Users of social networking sites should avoid personal opinions or negative comments that are not 100% factual and or statements that may harm a person's image or reputation." Use the litmus test to gauge whether the comment is appropriate to post by asking yourself, "Would my mother approve?"

Trademark

The improper use of trademarks on social networking platforms as well as the Internet at large has been a growing concern for years. A trademark includes any word, name, symbol, device, or a combination of these used, or with the intent to be used to identify and distinguish one company from another. A trademark is a brand name much like your Twitter username.

Because anyone can visit Twitter.com and register a username, cybersquatting has become a common practice. Cybersquatting is when a trademark owned by another party is used to make a profit. Twitter's terms and service specifically prohibits this practice. Use of another's trademark may result in trademark infringement.

A well-thought-out username is a great way to brand and differentiate yourself from the competition. Equally important is considering your username and the legal implications you might face if it is similar to a trademarked brand, product, or company.

8

Advanced Twitter Techniques

Once you have mastered the Twitter basics and have an understanding of @replies, URLs, and basic hashtags such as #followfriday, you are ready to dive into advanced Twitter strategies and techniques. Just like Twitter basics, the best way to learn is by diving right in.

Keywords

Just like search engine optimization (SEO) for Web sites, keywords are equally important for effective tweets on Twitter. Depending on your marketing strategy and business plan for using Twitter, it is important to do your research on other Twitter users and businesses who are working within your industry. Visit blogs, Web sites, and professional industry-related organization Web sites to learn about trending topics, buzzwords, and other pertinent information.

Conversely, it is equally important to effectively use keywords as a part of your real-time Twitter search. Understanding what your customers or potential customers are talking about on Twitter can help you engage them in a timely manner with customer service and with business savvy.

While updating my new domain, www.blogging4jobs. com, my husband, @SoonerExecRec, and I ran into a situation where our FTP upload was not working. After an hour of frustration and rereading the instruction manual multiple times, I tweeted my frustration out to the Twitterverse. My tweet included the keywords "wordpress" and "godaddy." Almost immediately, five tweeps either direct messaged me or sent an @reply to my attention to offer assistance, advice, or a paid service. Luckily, @GoDaddyGuy also saw my tweet for help. A phone call and fifteen minutes later, my wordpress problem was solved.

Twitter Integration Strategies

Having one voice and one image on multiple social media platforms can be a challenge for business. One way to allow for brand consistency and effective time management is to integrate your Twitter posts to other platforms. With a few clicks of the mouse, your Tweets can easily be integrated to other social media platforms such as LinkedIn, MySpace, and Facebook.

To integrate your Twitter posts to Facebook, visit the site www.twitter.com/wigits and select "Integrate Twitter to Facebook" and follow the prompts from there. If you have a MySpace profile or Blogger page you can promote your Twitter account with a customized widget. This can be done by visiting the above site and selecting the MySpace or Blogger options.

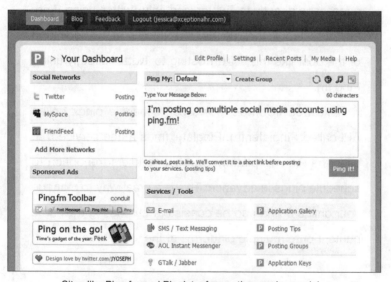

Sites like Ping.fm and Pinglater.fm are time saving social
media strategies for multiple platforms.

You can integrate your Twitter posts to LinkedIn by adding your Twitter address, www.twitter.com/yourusername, to your LinkedIn profile. This can be done by adding your Twitter profile address to your main profile page under "My Web sites." LinkedIn allows each LinkedIn user to list three separate Web sites.

Ping.fm is another tool to add to the social media arsenal. Ping.fm users can easily deliver a single post across more than forty social media platforms including Twitter, Facebook, LinkedIn, MySpace, Plaxo, Bebo, FeedFriend, and more. Ping.fm also allows for users to post to a specific service using a single service by prefixing your message with a service trigger. For example, to send a message directly to Twitter, and only Twitter, using Ping.fm, a user would include the "@tt" symbol at the beginning of the post like this, "@tt Posting to Twitter directly using Ping.fm."

Like SocialOomph, users can schedule pings on an API called Pinglater.fm. Pinglater.fm is a free service that uses the Ping.fm platform but allows users the option to schedule pings in advance. This is a great way to manage your online brand and be consistent by posting the same content onto multiple platforms at the same time.

Accelerated Organic Growth

While I encourage organic growth to gain creditability, follower count, and trust on Twitter, it is important to organize and target your efforts. A great tool I recommend to help grow your follower count and increase site traffic is

TweetAdder. TweetAdder.com is a third-party application that helps companies and individuals target and build your online Twitter rolodex using an automated system where the user designates the search and follower criteria. Users can create location-based searches, targeted searches using Twitter bios, import other Twitter accounts' followers, and designate keyword search terms to add followers to your specifications.

One of the best features of TweetAdder is that account holders can increase their follower account 24 hours a day, 7 days a week using a method that is slow, natural, and at a methodical pace. While the service isn't free, for some the cost may be worth it, starting at $55.00 for one account or unlimited profiles for $188.00. With over 27 million Twitter users and multiple social media platforms to manage, businesses should take advantage of every opportunity to automate the process while maintaining an authentic business and professional self.

Marketer Giovanni Gallucci, @giovanni, uses sites like TweetAdder to help accelerate and automate the marketing processes for businesses. Giovanni is a creative marketing and social media genius who works with businesses to help grow and develop using social media strategies. One of Giovanni's most recent projects involved consulting with public relations firm Moroch Entertainment and Angelika Movie Theatres where he developed a social media scavenger hunt to promote several free prereleased movie screenings. Giovanni and others sent out tweets and posts through multiple social media channels leading scavenger hunt participants to a Twitter account that they were asked to follow. Upon following, participants received an automatic direct message leading to several blogs and other sites instructing them to leave comments or subscribe to mailing lists before being led to a site where they downloaded a free screening pass PDF.

Giovanni and his team were able to track the success of the scavenger hunt and PDF download using Google Analytics. Because the movie screening promotion was accomplished using social media platforms and blogs, the cost associated with promotion was time and labor during set up. Of those who attended the free screening, 34 percent were scavenger hunt participants. Angelika Movie Theatres was able to attract a new and different audience throughout multiple geographic markets as a result of the scavenger hunt promotion in contrast to their more traditional marketing strategies that include localized radio and events promotions.

Using Hashtags

Hashtags are a great way to stay up-to-date on the latest topics, comments, opinions, and key takeaways at special events and conferences. Hashtags can allow conference speakers to receive immediate feedback about a presentation or luncheon. Businesses can also use hashtags as a way to generate interest and fun for a large event like a Tweetup. In May 2009, three colleagues and I hosted an OKC Tweetup at @chefrp's Iguana Mexican Grill in Oklahoma City, Oklahoma. Tweeps were encouraged to tweet before, during, and after the event using our designated hashtag, #okctweetup. To generate even more interest, we developed a series of YouTube videos that incorporated the hashtag into the tweeted video. The videos and hashtag also served as a form of promotion and drove traffic to our Web site, www.okctweetup.com.

Timing Is Everything

Just like determining your target demographic, it is important to determine the best time to tweet and grab your target market's attention. According to research conducted over an eight-week period by Matt Galloway, @mattgalloway, for the state of Oklahoma between March 29, and May 31, 2009, the geography behind your audience should influence your online marketing strategy.

Dubbed the Oklahoma Twitter Census, Matt's work determined that the state's Twitter population is between 31,000–47,000 — meaning that 1 in 100 Oklahomans is active on Twitter. His research indicated that the college and university towns of Norman and Stillwater had glaringly different tweeting time trends versus the Oklahoma metropolitan areas of Tulsa and Oklahoma City. University and college towns frequent Twitter between noon and late evening while Oklahoma City and Tulsa's peak tweeting times were between the hours of 9:00 a.m. and 6:00 p.m.

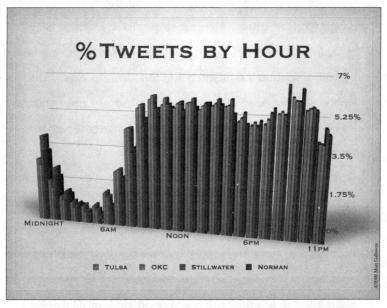

Just like television and radio broadcasting, it is important to understand when your target market is logged on to Twitter. This graph shows that university campuses in Oklahoma use Twitter later in the day.

It was also no surprise that the large populated areas from within the state had a larger percentage of Twitter users.

Engaging Power Users

As you begin to build your follower base and develop

relationships with people within your industry and your geographic region, engaging influential tweeps or power users is another great way to improve Twitter techniques and develop relationships with social media high rollers.

The Twitter community is a community of giving, reciprocity, and relationships. Aligning yourself with social

> @blogging4jobs You might be interested in checking out MyWorkster.com. Feel free to let me know if you have any questions as well!
>
> 2:52 PM Jul 29th from web in reply to blogging4jobs

Taylor Crane, the voice for the @MyWorkster twitter account engaged me with an @reply message which led to me interviewing him for this book and also highlighting My Workster on my blog, Blogging4Jobs.

media influencers is an important part of successful social media networking.

My Workster, @MyWorkster, is a relative newbie to the social media world. Myworkster.com launched in early 2009 and is an affinity social media community and platform that provides colleges, universities, students, alumni, and businesses a way to develop relationships and advertise job openings. @MyWorkster joined Twitter in July 2009 with a targeted strategy that involves using keyword searches as a way to establish relationships, developing targeted relationships with power users to drive their online brand, and the launch of an online viral video campaign using blogs, Twitter, and Digg.

Taylor Crane, who manages the My Workster Twitter account, contacted me in July 2009 via an @reply using

Search.Twitter to search for keyword jobs. My Workster, which has ninety-seven followers, seeks to grow their Twitter following and continue to promote their business to job seekers, colleges and universities, and recruiters.

Proceed with Caution

I cannot emphasize enough the importance of having a specific marketing plan. One of the advantages to the Internet is that it levels the marketing playing field for both large and small businesses—allowing them an audience of millions. Because it takes only minutes to create a Twitter profile and upload a picture, it is easy to jump right in without proper business preparation. Habitat is an unfortunate example. Habitat is a trendy furniture store located throughout Europe. Their United Kingdom division opened a Twitter account, @HabitatUK, with the goal of marketing and promoting their sales and specials.

@HabitatUK and their use of hashtags became
a classic example of a Twitter don't.

In a matter of days, @HabitatUK fell under world scrutiny with the use of trending hashtags in their tweets. The hashtags in question included #apple, #trueblood, and #mousavi among others. These hashtag topics were used by @HabitatUK in an attempt to broaden their reach. Instead, Habitat was the topic of blogs, news articles, and agencies; and Twitter saddled them with another common hashtag meant for spammers on Twitter: #spam.

In response to the increased negative publicity, Habitat issued a response along with a link that directed tweeps to a public apology featured on socialmediatoday.com.

Achieving Twittertopia in 30 Minutes a Day (or Less)

Create a Marketing Plan

Like any public relations or marketing project, you must have a plan with a goal in mind. Outline your intentions, the goals you wish to achieve, and the timeline for your results. Like any business strategy, you must have a solid plan with actionable results along with a realistic timeline. If you bought this book with the intention that Twitter will increase your sales by 50 percent and grow your market share in two weeks, I am sorry to tell you that these goals likely will not happen.

Putting a solid strategy into action will take at least six months to see or measure actionable results. Because social media and the Internet are ever-evolving and always changing, the window to plan your attack is very small.

The upside is that six months is a very short time when you consider that most effective change management strategies take eighteen to twenty-four months or longer to implement full-cycle.

I strongly encourage you to grow your Twitter following purely and organically with real content—which is why I included the Habitat example in this book. Because social media is a relatively young marketing concept and it changes at great speed, it is very likely that, much like MySpace, tweeps will move onto the next big thing in the future. This is one of the reasons I enjoy social media. Social media, and their use and strategies, are much like the Twitter stream that is always moving and ever-changing.

Learn and Observe

Habitat serves as an example for many. Their mistake not only teaches us about organic growth but also the importance of understanding each different social media platform, its nuances, and proven strategies before you jump right in. I recommend that you follow the tweeps I've listed in this book as well as your competitors, local businesses, successful businesses, and others who have felt the sting of what happens when we don't learn and observe.

Blogs are a great way to research and learn about best practices and strategies from businesses and experts who are firmly planted at the forefront of the social media industry. I recommend subscribing to blog feeds to receive up-to-the-minute information from these social media and business influencers and power users.

The Central Oklahoma Humane Society, a nonprofit located in Oklahoma City has received national recognition for their use of social media as a way to market their services, promote their business, and find volunteers as well as homes or foster homes for pets. In addition to their blog at www.okhumaneblog.com, the Central Oklahoma Humane Society uses Twitter, Facebook, MySpace, Flickr, and many other social media platforms.

In April 2009, @okhumane used Twitter as a way to generate support, inform the public, and promote the passage of HB 1332 in the Oklahoma State Senate. @okhumane led supporters and opposers to the Oklahoma Humane Society Blog where comments were not censored and sought to provide the most current legislative news for blog readers. @okhumane has received national attention for its social media efforts, speaking at several conferences across the United States.

Join the Conversation

Once you have done your homework, it is okay to dive right in. Know that you will make some mistakes, but hopefully with your careful preparation, research, and planning, you will outshine the rest.

Start out slow. I recommend posting five to ten tweets a day as you gain followers over the first two weeks. As you become more comfortable with Twitter, experiment with new third-party applications, texting updates to Twitter, and iPhone applications as well as other social media platforms.

Integrate on Multiple Platforms

For new users, Twitter can be overwhelming, but if you stick to your marketing plan and do your research, it will not be long before others look to you for advice and best practices. Share your message and success and broaden your potential customer scope by integrating your tweets onto other platforms using tools like SocialOomph, HootSuite, and even Pinglater.fm. This integration saves time and cuts down on repetitive comments and posts on sites like Facebook, LinkedIn, Ping, and MySpace. It is important to remember that you cannot schedule live engagement with your clients, customers, peers, and target audience.

Schedule Your Day

Use tools like SocialOomph to schedule your tweets for the day. Make sure to target your tweets at the highest peak traffic times for your audience and vary the times in which you post. If you schedule a tweet for 11:15 a.m., schedule another for 12:31 p.m., not 12:15 p.m. Your audience wants to see your true, authentic self, and as a business, you make the most of your valuable time while appearing available and accessible to everyone.

I also recommend using other third-party applications such as TweetDeck to create groups and keyword searches and to manage your accounts using mobile technologies. Other services like TweetBeep make monitoring your brand or trending topics much easier with e-mail updates that you control.

Tweet:	New Blog Post: Breaking into HR http://is.gd/20tLj
Shorten URLs	
	50 characters entered.
Save As Draft:	☐ Save this tweet text as a draft that can be reused later.
Publish When:	☐ Publish right now (will be published within 60 seconds) ☐ Publish _____ hour(s) ▼ from now Or publish at this exact time: 08/10/2009 09:17 am 🔲12 mm/dd/yyyy hh:mm am/pm - Change your date format
Recurrence:	*With TweetLater Professional, you can schedule recurring tweets (with spinnable text) and @replies, plus the 12 tweets per hour limit does not apply. Make your tweeting even more effective and productive.*
Account(s):	blogging4jobs xceptionalhr _RSSFeed blogging4jobs Publish tweet on these accounts ⓦ

TweetLater is an essential tool in managing your Twitter account in under 30 minutes a day.

Each morning, I log on to SocialOomph to schedule my tweets, which takes roughly ten minutes. Later that afternoon, using my iPhone, I check Tweetie for any @

replies or direct messages that I need to address, making comments as necessary for a total of less than five minutes. Again, as the workday begins to wind down, I log on to TweetDeck or TweetVisor to check in again, making comments, engaging others, and answering any messages for a total of fifteen minutes. If I come across an article or blog post I find particularly interesting, I highlight the post as a favorite, flagging it to read later. And when I have some downtime either while waiting in line at the bank or in traffic, I will catch up on my flagged favorite tweets and posts that caught my attention.

Use your Outlook calendar to plan your day. Schedule yourself several reoccurring ten- to thirty-minute appointments once or twice a day to ensure that you take the time to engage your audience on Twitter. Just because you don't have a mobile device doesn't mean you can't quickly respond to customer comments and questions. Laptop and desktop computers using third-party applications like TweetDeck and others are great time-saving tools.

Most importantly, when scheduling tweets, your content is of the utmost importance. I recommend planning your tweets by week, sprinkling it strategically. In the appendix is a weekly Brand Plan to organize your tweets, upcoming events or topics you want to highlight, and the times you wish to engage your audience.

Engage Others

Engage customers new and established, those within your industry as well as those you admire. Twitter is a great way to receive real-time feedback and opinions from followers. Seek input from your audience for things like blog post topics, advice from mentors, and asked questions. Twitter has opened my eyes to new resources and people and has broadened my scope of business. Plus, it is fun and exciting to be on the cutting edge.

Twitter is an excellent way to promote your business through referrals or customer testimonial videos. Creativity is king. Don't be afraid to upload a new video or post. Yes, there is risk, but there is also reward.

Appendix

Brand Plan Questionnaire

1. What is the age range of the customer who wants my brand, product, or service?

2. Which gender would be more interested in my brand, product, or service?

3. What is the income level of my potential customers?

4. What education status do they have?

5. What is their marital or family status?

6. Is this a product or service they need, or is it a luxury item?

7. How will the consumer use this product or service?

8. What will draw or attract the customer to this product or service?

Brand Plan

- What do I wish to accomplish as a long-term goal or strategy over three to five years?
- What do I wish to accomplish as a short-term goal or strategy over six months to two years?
- My Mission Statement for my company or place of business is the following:

List the special features or benefits of your product or service:

1. _____

2. _____

3. _____

4. _____

5. _____

List how you are currently marketing or promoting your product over the next six months and the cost associated with those efforts:

1. _____

2. _____

3. _____

4. _____

5. _____

Twitter Brand Plan

My business strategy for using Twitter is:

_____

_____

_____

_____

_____

_____

_____

_____

_____

_____

I will accomplish this the following ways:

1. _____

2. _____

3. _____

4. _____

5. _____

I plan on cross-promoting my product, service, or brand using the following social media tools or other strategies (include dates and points of reference):

My 14 Day Twitter Strategy is the following:

I have scheduled time in my datebook or Outlook calendar to manage Twitter daily.

_____yes _____ no

Day 1_____

Day 2_____

Day 3_____

Day 4_____

Day 5_____

Day 6_____

Day 7_____

Day 8_____

Day 9_____

Day 10_____

Day 11_____

Day 12_____

Day 13_____

Day 14_____

What were my results? (include successes, failures, and takeaways):

_____

_____

_____

_____

_____

Additional Comments:

_____

_____

_____

_____

_____

_____

_____

_____

_____

_____

_____

_____

_____

_____

_____

_____

_____

_____

_____

_____

Twitter Glossary

Applications–Twitter is written in open code that allows others to create tools and other sites that work with Twitter. Examples include Tweetvisor, TweetDeck, and WeFollow.

At Reply (@)–The "@" sign is used when speaking directly to another Twitter user when posting a tweet. Place the @ sign in front of the Twitter username or moniker ("@blogging4jobs" username is "blogging4jobs").

Auto Follow–When another tweep automatically follows you after being followed.

Bio–Biography section on your Twitter profile that is available to the general public where you can include your personal information and background on your profile. This information is searchable on Twitter Search.

Blog–A type of Web site with regular entries in reverse chronological order with topics and posts about a variety of topics allowing for reader comments.

Direct Message (DM)–Direct form of communication written in 140 characters that only you and the direct message recipient can view.

Follower–Those who are interested in you and your tweet stream and follow you and view your tweets.

#FollowFriday–Twitter users use this hashtag to recommend followers to other tweets each Friday. It is easily searchable using Twitter Search.

Following–What you do when you are interested in another Twitter user, allowing for their tweets to be part of your Twitter stream (Information Stream).

Hashtag–The "#" sign which allows Twitter users to group their tweet with a particular event or conversation. The hashtag makes it easier to search for that particular conversation on Twitter Search (http:// search.twitter.com). The hashtag is used like this: #okctweetup.

Link–Tiny URL for Twitter Glossary http://tinyurl com/2f9pq7

Retweet (RT)–Repeating or reposting an interesting tweet from another Twitter user. This is commonly referred to as "going viral" and allows the retweeted user increased exposure on the World Wide Web. It is considered the greatest form of Twitter flattery.

RSS Feed–A common method used to view blogs, article topics, writers, or Twitter keyword searches (http:// search.twitter.com allows this functionality).

Tweeple–Twitter people, Twitter members, Twitter users.

Tweeps–Twitterites who follow each other from one social media/network to another.

Tweet–Not only a message on Twitter but another term for a Twitter user (often jokingly mistaken as a Twit).

Tweet(ing)–The act of posting to Twitter.

Tweetup–A Twitter meetup or networking meeting for face-to-face interaction offline among tweeple.

Twewbie–A Twitter newbie. Someone who is new to Twitter.

Twitizens–Nickname for Twitter citizens who are registered users of Twitter.com.

Twitterholic–A person who is addicted to Twitter. Also a Web site showing top twitter rankings (http:// twitterholic.com).

Twitterphobic–Someone who dislikes or fears Twitter to some degree.

Twitter Stream–Stream of tweets and flow of information on Twitter.com. Your Twitter stream includes the updates of those you choose to follow in real time.

Twitterverse–The body of the Twitter universe, a community. Similar to a blogosphere. Also known as Twitterville, Tweet Nation, Tweetopolis, Twitterworld.

Web Widget–A stand-alone function you can embed in other applications.

Vlog–Also known as video blogging. Entries are made regularly and often combine embedded videos or a video link with supporting text, images, and other data.

Resources

Allbusiness.com. May 2009.

Bit.ly. June 2009.

Brogan, Chris. www.chrisbrogan.com. July 2009

Cashmore, Pete. www.Mashable.com. June 2009.

Donovan, Lisa. "Tweet about apartment mold draws lawsuit." www.suntimes.com. July 2009.

Givens, Lotoicha. "Defamation and Social Media." www.iplaw101.com. August 2009.

Gallucci, Giovanni. http://gallucci.net/. July 2009.

Jobangels.org. May 2009. +

Leggio, Jennifer. "Cool Tools—What is Your Twitter Grade?" http://blogs.zdnet.com/feeds/?p=208. May 2009.

Levy, Steven. "Twitter: Is Brevity the Next Big Thing?" Newsweek. http://www.newsweek.com/id/35289. 2007.

Lobatot, Ryan. "What's in a Username?" www.mcafeetaft.com. June 2009.

Malik, Om. "A brief history of Twitter." www.gigaom.com. Feb. 2009.

McCarthy, Caroline. "No surprise here: Oprah appearance huge for Twitter." News.cnet.com. April 2009.

Moses, Asher. "Mumbai Attacks Reported Live on Twitter, Flickr." http://www.theage.com.au/news/technology/web/mumbai-attacks-live-on-twitter-flickr/2008/11/27/1227491713487.html. November 27, 2008.

Murnahan, Mark Aaron. www.awebguy.com. June 2009.

Ping.fm. June 2009.

Pinglater.fm. July 2009.

Postman, Joel. "Live Tweeting Requires Ethical and Legal Considerations." www.socialmediatoday.com. July 2009.

Pulver, Jeff. www.jeffpulver.com. June 2009.

Quantcast.com. July 2009.

Revolution Magazine. "The 100 Most Mentioned Brands on Twitter." May 2009.

Rowse, Darren. "Twitip." www.Twitip.com. July 2009.

Schawbel, Dan. www.personalbrandingblog.com. July 2009.

Sexton, Koka. www.kokasexton.com. June 2009.

SocialOomph.com. September 2009.

Smith, Mari. www.marismith.com. June 2009.

Sutton, Wayne. www.socialwayne.com. May 2009.

Tipereth. "How not to use Twitter : HabitatUK as a case study." www.socialmediatoday.com. June 2009.

TweetAdder.com. July 2009.

Tweetbeep.com. May 2009.

TweetDeck.com. June 2009.

Tweetie.com. July 2009.

TweetVisor.com. May 2009.

Twellow.com. April 2009.

Twictionary: The Dictionary for Twitter. http://twictionary.
    pbwiki.com/. March 2009.

TwitPic.com. August 2009.

Twitscoop.com. May 2009.

Twitter.com. April-August 2009.

Twitterfon.com. July 2009.

Twittergrader.com. May 2009.

SearchTwitter.com. May 2009.

Vaughn, Randy. www.marketingtwins.com. May 2009.

Wikipedia.com. April-July 2009.

Wilson, Chris. www.freshpeel.com.

Using Twitter as a Frenzy Promotion Tool. March 2009.

Index

About the Author

Jessica Miller-Merrell, SPHR, is an author, new mother, and human resources professional with a passion for recruiting and all things social media.

Jessica has over ten years of experience in human resources and recruiting and is the owner and president of Xceptional HR, LLC, a leading social media recruitment strategy and human resource firm. Jessica is a leading voice in the human resource and social media community and regularly speaks about how small- to medium-sized businesses can use social media to develop an online brand and grow their client and candidate pools. She holds the designation of Senior Professional in Human Resources, and her blog and online Web show, Blogging4Jobs, is one of the most recognizable job-seeker resources on the Internet.

Xceptional HR provides a range of services and resources to help companies with recruiting and recruitment strategies, human resource consulting, social media campaigns, and marketing. To learn more about Jessica or her company, please visit www.jessicamillermerrell. com or www.blogging4jobs.com.